40 FANTASTIC RECIPES

THE
HEINZ TOMATO KETCHUP
COOKBOOK

PAUL HARTLEY

ABSOLUTE PRESS

In association with
www.breakfastandbrunch.com

First published in Great Britain
in 2007
by **Absolute Press**
Scarborough House
29 James Street West
Bath BA1 2BT
Phone 44 (0) 1225 316013
Fax 44 (0) 1225 445836
E-mail info@absolutepress.co.uk
Website www.absolutepress.co.uk

Publisher
Jon Croft
Commissioning Editor
Meg Avent
Designer
Matt Inwood
Publishing Assistant
Meg Devenish
Photography
Peter Cassidy
Props Stylist
Cynthia Inions
Food Stylist
Claire Ptak

Reprinted 2007, 2008.

© Absolute Press, 2007

Text copyright
© Paul Hartley, 2007

A catalogue record of this book
is available from the British Library

ISBN 9781904573760

Printed and bound by
Oriental Press, Dubai.

CONTENTS

6 THE HEINZ TOMATO KETCHUP RECIPE COLLECTION

8 Spicy Ginger & Orange Chicken

9 Tuna Croquettes

10 Schnitzel with Noodles

11 Tearing Sharing Focaccia

14 Clam & Tomato Gnocchi

15 Turkey Meatballs with Tomato Sauce

16 Perfect Prawn Cocktail

18 Bloody Mary Macaroni

19 Herby Scones with Tomato & Feta

20 Sticky Chicken Kebabs

21 Golden Egg Boat Curry

24 Moroccan Fish Tagine

26 Breakfast Tomato & Potato Waffles

27 Coconut, Chilli & Squash Soup

28 Cauliflower Fritters with Sweet Chilli Dip

32 Andalucian Fish Pie

33 Greek Lamb Pasties with Fresh Oregano

35 Smoky Joe's Tomato Chutney

37 Red Thai Duck Curry

38 Wild Mushroom Diablo

40 Lamb & Mint Brunch Burgers with Riverside Salsa

44 TK & Passionfruit Ice Cream

46 Pastrami, Rocket & Red Chard Salad with Rye Croûtons

48 Bangers & Mash with Red Onion Gravy

50 Chargrilled Brill with Tomato & Dill Butter

51 TK Parmesan Straws

52 Gazpacho with Anchovy Croûtons

56 Goulash with Horseradish & Herb Dumplings

58 Chorizo & Summer Vegetable Omelette

59 TK Fiery Barbecue Marinade

60 Veggie Moussaka

61 Rib Steaks with Stilton Sauce

64 Pork & Apple Meatloaf

65 Roasted Red Pepper Salad

66 Fragrant Martini Mussels

68 Sherried Duck with Watercress Mash

70 Balsamic Barbecue Ribs

72 Pork Sweet & Sour

73 Spinach, Pepper and Mushroom Terrine

74 Tomato-Crusted Lamb Rack with Baby Vegetables

76 KETCHUP TIMELINE

79 ACKNOWLEDGEMENTS

THE
HEINZ TOMATO KETCHUP
RECIPE COLLECTION

SPICY GINGER & ORANGE CHICKEN

Just a delicious chicken casserole with heavenly exotic flavours.

SERVES 6

6 chicken portions (allow about 225g per person)
1 tablespoon golden syrup
2 tablespoons Heinz Tomato Ketchup
1 heaped teaspoon finely grated fresh ginger
1 level teaspoon ground mixed spice
1 level teaspoon ground cinnamon
200ml freshly squeezed orange juice (about 2 medium
   juicy oranges)
Sea salt and freshly ground black pepper

Preheat the oven to 180C/350F/Gas4. Put the chicken portions into a large ovenproof dish.

Mix together the golden syrup, ketchup, mixed spice and cinnamon to make a paste. Gradually stir in the orange juice and finally add the ginger, mix well and spoon over the chicken portions.

Cover the dish with foil and cook for 30 minutes scooping the juices up and over the chicken a few times. Then remove the foil and cook for a further 10 minutes.

Lift out the chicken and keep warm. Pour the remaining juices into a saucepan and boil rapidly to reduce it by half making it thicker and spoonable. Serve the chicken doused in the spicy ginger and orange sauce. Scrummy with roasted sweet potato wedges and a simple endive salad.

WHY '57'?

THE STORY GOES THAT Henry Heinz was riding the New York railway one day when he noticed an advertisement for a shoe company boasting a variety of 21 styles. He considered this and started to count all the products that the Heinz company was producing. He concluded that there were about 57 (there were actually far more, but the numbers '5' and '7' had a lucky charm for him!). Hence the birth of the mark '57 VARIETIES'.

TUNA CROQUETTES

Breadcrumb-encrusted tuna with parsley, potatoes and tomato ketchup.

SERVES 6 (MAKES 12 CROQUETTES)

600g potatoes, peeled and cut into chunks
1 free-range egg
25g unsalted butter, softened
450g fresh tuna steaks about 2cm thick
1 teaspoon anchovy essence
2 tablespoons Heinz Tomato Ketchup
2 tablespoons chopped fresh parsley
Freshly milled black pepper
Seasoned flour for coating
2 eggs, beaten
Fresh white breadcrumbs

Cook the potatoes in boiling salted water for 15–20 minutes, until tender. Drain, return them to the pan and mash together with one egg and the butter.

In the meantime, grill the tuna steaks under a medium heat for 3–4 minutes on each side until just cooked through. Leave to cool.

In a large bowl spread out the mash adding the tuna broken into small flakes. In a small bowl mix together the anchovy essence, ketchup and parsley and dollop it onto the tuna mash. Season with plenty of black pepper. Fold all the ingredients in together well – a soft spatula is perfect for this.

Using wet hands to stop the mixture sticking to you mould into croquettes, a bit like thick homemade hamburgers, approximately 100g each. Dip the croquettes into seasoned flour, then into beaten egg and finally into the breadcrumbs, making sure they are evenly coated. Chill in the fridge for half and hour to set the breadcrumbs.

You can either shallow fry or deep-fry the fishcakes when ready. Cook in batches for 4–5 minutes until the coating is golden and crispy. Drain on kitchen paper. Great served with a leafy green salad, wedges of lemon, good tartare sauce or sweet chilli dipping sauce.

Among the first of the '57 VARIETIES' products to be introduced by Heinz:

1869 **Horseradish**	1870 **Chow chow pickle**	1870 **Sauerkraut in crocks**
1870 **Sour gherkins**	1870 **Sour onions**	1873 **Vinegar**
1870 **Mixed sour pickles**	1870 **Prepared mustard**	1876 **Tomato ketchup**

SCHNITZEL WITH NOODLES

Pork fillet beaten wafer thin nestling under a pile of tomato noodles.

SERVES 2

1 piece of pork fillet, 300–400g
1 free-range egg
50g white breadcrumbs (blitzed stale ciabatta works
    really well)
Sunflower oil for frying
2 sheets medium egg noodles
3 tablespoon Heinz Tomato Ketchup
2 teaspoons light soy sauce
2 lemon wedges

Cut the pork fillet in half across the centre. Using a sharp knife cut down the length of each piece making sure the knife only goes $3/4$ of the way through the meat so that you can open it like a butterfly. Using a meat hammer beat it out teasing it from the centre outwards until it is no more than $1/2$cm thick overall.

Prepare 2 shallow dishes into which the schnitzels will fit. Break the egg into one dish and whisk it up. Spread the breadcrumbs out in the other dish. Dunk each schnitzel first into the egg and then into the breadcrumbs making sure it is well coated with each. Place on greaseproof paper and chill in the fridge for one hour to set the coating. If you skip the chilling the coating will fall off when cooked.

When you are ready to cook bring a pan of water to the boil, add the dried noodles, pop on the lid and remove the pan from the heat. They don't need cooking they just need to rehydrate in the hot water. Using a fork swizzle the noodles around a few times until they loosen and swell a little – about 5 minutes. Drain, add the soy sauce and ketchup and again using a fork make sure they are really well mixed. Leave aside and keep warm.

Heat one tablespoon of oil in a large frying pan over a medium to high heat and add one schnitzel. Cook for 3–4 minutes on each side until the coating is golden and crispy. Keep warm while you cook the second schnitzel adding a little more oil if required.

Lay the schnitzels on warmed plates and place the noodles half on, half off, one side of the schnitzel and garnish with a lemon wedge. This dish originates in Vienna where the meat is served very thin and very big. Guten appetit!

TEARING SHARING FOCACCIA

Ham and cheese bread marbled with tomato ketchup.

MAKES I LOAF

2 teaspoons dried yeast
300ml water
500g strong white flour
$1^1/_2$ teaspoons salt
Olive oil
2 tablespoons Heinz Tomato Ketchup
50g Cheddar cheese, crumbled
60g smoked ham, roughly diced
Pinch of coarse salt
8 little rosemary top sprigs

In a small bowl sprinkle the yeast into 200ml of the water. Leave for 5 minutes and then stir to dissolve. Sieve the flour and salt into a large bowl, make a well in the centre and pour in the yeast mixture and 3 tablespoons of olive oil. Mix the flour by working from the outside into the centre and add the remaining water to make a sticky dough. Turn out onto a lightly floured surface and knead for about 10 minutes until the dough is smooth and elastic. Put into a lightly oiled bowl, cover with a tea towel and leave at room temperature until the dough has doubled in size – up to 2 hours.

Knock back or deflate the dough by pressing down in the centre with your knuckles. Divide it into two rounds and circle the dough between your hands tucking it in and under as you go round – you need to do this for about 5 minutes. Leave to rest for 10 minutes.

Gently roll out each half to create roughly 20cm rounds. Put one round on a lightly oiled baking sheet and spread with ketchup, then scatter with the ham and cheese adding 4 good dollops of ketchup for the final flourish. Seal the 'sandwich' of dough with the other round and pinch together round the edges. Cover loosely with a tea towel and leave to prove for about 30 minutes, until doubled in size.

Preheat the oven to 200C/400F/Gas 6.

Press gently into the surface of the dough with your fingertips to make little dimples, pop in the mini sprigs of rosemary, then scatter with sea salt and drizzle with a little more olive oil. Bake for 30–40 minutes until golden. Remove from the oven and drizzle straight away with a little more olive oil and serve warm to tear and share.

1880-1905 1889-1894 1887-1895 1889-1910 1906-1910

CLAM & TOMATO GNOCCHI

Baby clams, vine tomatoes and potato pasta all in a luscious cream sauce.

SERVES 2–3

500g fresh clams
2 ripe vine tomatoes
500g pack fresh gnocchi
75g frozen petits pois
200ml double cream
1 tablespoon Heinz Tomato Ketchup
1 tablespoon freshly grated Parmesan
Salt and freshly ground black pepper
Few sprigs of fresh dill

First prepare the clams by washing them thoroughly in cold water, discarding any broken or open ones. Put the clams into a large pan over a medium heat, add a splash of water and put the lid on. Over a 6–8 minute period shake the pan once or twice until all the clams are fully open. Remove them with a slotted spoon, leaving the milky liquid in the pan to add to the sauce later. Remove all the meat from the shells leaving 6 per person in their shells for garnish.

Put the tomatoes in a bowl, pour over boiling water and leave for 1 minute. Remove the tomatoes with a slotted spoon, allow to cool slightly and then slide off the skins. Deseed and chop them, keeping any juice you can.

Place 2 pans of lightly salted water on to boil, one large and one small. Add the gnocchi to the larger pan and the peas to the smaller one and cook them both for 3–4 minutes. Pour the cream into another small pan, add the ketchup, 2 tablespoons of the reserved clam juice, the Parmesan and tomatoes and warm gently for a few minutes. Taste and season accordingly with salt and pepper. Add the shelled clams at the last minute just to warm them through.

Drain the gnocchi and peas in a colander and divide between warmed plates. Pour the creamy tomato sauce over the top, arrange the shell on clams and scatter over some tiny sprigs of dill before serving.

ATTACK OF THE KILLER TOMATOES WAS A 1978 FILM THAT SPAWNED THREE SEQUELS!

TURKEY MEATBALLS WITH TOMATO SAUCE

Minced turkey breast enhanced with a hot fresh tomato sauce.

SERVES 4–6

500g minced turkey meat (ask your butcher if you don't
   have a mincer)
1 onion, grated
1 free-range egg, beaten
100g breadcrumbs
3 tablespoons Heinz Tomato Ketchup
1 tablespoon flat leaf parsley, chopped
40g Parmesan or Pecorino cheese, grated
Salt and black pepper
Olive oil

For the tomato sauce
1 tablespoon sunflower oil
$1/2$ onion, finely diced
4 tomatoes, peeled seeded and diced
Dash of Worcestershire sauce
$1/2$ teaspoon dried mixed herbs
1 tablespoon Heinz Tomato Ketchup
Salt and pepper
4 torn basil leaves plus extra for garnish

Put the turkey meat into a large bowl and add the onion, egg, breadcrumbs, ketchup, parsley and cheese. Season with salt and pepper and then using your hands (really good and squidgy this!) mix all the ingredients well together. Form into balls in the palm of your hand, about the size of a golf ball – having wet hands prevents it all from sticking to you. Place the meatballs on greaseproof paper on a plate and chill for up to 1 hour. You should get about 20 meatballs from this mixture.

In the meantime prepare the fresh tomato sauce by frying the onions in the oil until transparent. Add the tomatoes to the pan with the Worcestershire sauce, herbs and ketchup then taste and season with salt and plenty of freshly ground black pepper. Cook the sauce gently for about 5 minutes until you have a pulp that still retains a good texture. Keep the sauce aside until you are ready to use it.

When ready preheat the oven to 180C/350F/Gas 4. Drizzle a baking tray with a little olive oil and put the meatballs into the tray. Swirl them round to coat with the oil and bake for 40 minutes until golden. Divide the meatballs onto plates for your lucky guests and spoon over the warmed tomato sauce, garnish with basil leaves and serve with homemade parsnip chips.

PERFECT PRAWN COCKTAIL

One of the great starters – prawns layered with a rich aurora sauce. Aurora is the rosy glow that just precedes the dawn This is a perfect sauce to serve with a prawn cocktail or a platter of smoked fish.

FOR 4 PEOPLE

For the salad
Crispy lettuce like iceberg, cos, romaine or little gem
2 ripe medium tomatoes, chopped
1 ripe avocado (only peel it when you are ready to use
    it as it will quickly discolour)
1kg fresh shell-on prawns, peeled, leaving 8 shell on
    for garnish (you can use peeled prawns, but they
    don't hold the same 'sea-fresh' flavour)
Parsley and lemon slices to garnish

For the Aurora sauce
4 tablespoons mayonnaise
3 tablespoons Heinz Tomato Ketchup
1 heaped teaspoon tomato purée
1 level teaspoon horseradish sauce
Good dash Worcestershire sauce
Salt and freshly ground white pepper (remember: black
    pepper for flavour and white pepper for heat)
1 teaspoon lemon juice
Zest of $\frac{1}{2}$ a lemon
Pinch smoked paprika

To make the aurora sauce mix all the ingredients together in a bowl and taste; then adjust the seasonings as required. Leave to stand in a cool place for at least half an hour so that the flavours can fuse, but make sure you serve at room temperature.

In a straight-sided, glass whisky tumbler put a layer of lettuce (about 1cm) then a layer of chopped tomato, more lettuce, a layer of prawns, a layer of sliced avocado, lettuce again and top with a good layer of prawns. Drizzle generously with the Aurora sauce and finish with a flourish of chopped parsley and a twist of lemon. Perfect.

BLOODY MARY MACARONI

Thick tubes of pasta married to a spicy vodka, tomato and celery sauce.

SERVES 4

For the sauce
1 medium onion, peeled and diced
Olive oil
1 x 400g tin chopped Italian plum tomatoes
100ml vodka
1 tablespoon sherry
2 tablespoons Heinz Tomato Ketchup
Few dashes of Worcestershire sauce
Dash of Tabasco Sauce
1/2 teaspoon celery salt
Freshly ground black pepper
1 teaspoon dried Italian herbs

400g macaroni
1 vegetable stock cube
Handful of torn basil
   leaves

In a large frying pan cook the onions in a little olive oil then add the rest of the sauce ingredients apart from the herbs. Turn up the heat and cook fairly rapidly until you can no longer smell alcohol in the steam and the sauce has thickened, this should take 8–10 minutes. Stir in the herbs, remove the pan from the heat and set aside.

Bring a pan of water to the boil, crumble in the stock cube and add the macaroni. Cook for 8–10 minutes or until the pasta is just al dente. Drain and drizzle with a little olive oil and season with black pepper.

Reheat the sauce if necessary, serve the macaroni in warmed bowls and pour over the sauce. Garnish with the basil leaves and serve with Parmesan shavings.

A WELL-TRAVELLED SAUCE

The word ketchup possibly has its origins in the Chinese word *ke-tsiap*, a pickled fish sauce, the savoury taste of which was down to the mingled flavours of spicy brine and fish. It travelled from China to Malaysia where it became *kechap*. It ventured onwards to Indonesia where it was *ketjap*. In the 17th-Century, Dutch and English sailors so enjoyed slathering their foods with it that they took it onboard with them, back to the West. They unveiled their booty once home, and the sauce drew comparisons with soy sauce

HERBY SCONES WITH TOMATO & FETA

Savoury scones for lunchtime soups or teatime munchies.

MAKES 10 SCONES

125g wholemeal flour
150g self-raising flour
1 level teaspoon baking powder
$\frac{1}{2}$ teaspoon mustard powder
Pinch paprika
2 tablespoons olive oil
150g Feta cheese
1 teaspoon chopped fresh thyme
1 teaspoon chopped fresh parsley
Handful black olives (about 8), pitted and chopped
3 tablespoons Heinz Tomato Ketchup
1 free-range egg
75ml milk

Preheat the oven to 220C/425F/Gas 7. You will need a 5–6cm cutter and a lightly greased baking tray.

Sieve the flours and baking powder into a large bowl and then add the mustard and paprika. Gradually add the olive oil and mix until you have a lumpy crumb mixture. Next add 100g of the Feta cheese in small cubes, the fresh herbs and the olives.

In a small bowl beat together the ketchup, eggs and milk and add this gradually to the flour mixture leaving a teaspoon or so for brushing later. Using your hands or a wooden spoon blend together to form a dough that is soft but not too sticky.

Flour a board and roll out the dough until it is about 2.5cm thick. Cut out 10 rounds, re-rolling and using up the odd bits. Lay the rounds on the baking tray and brush each with the reserved egg and milk mixture. Crumble the remaining 50g of Feta cheese on top of them and put into the top part of the oven to bake for 12–15 minutes or until they are golden. Cool a little on a wire rack before tucking in.

and with Worcestershire sauce. The sauce was modified over the years. British alternatives included the brine of pickled mushrooms, anchovies, oysters, and walnuts – these were often quite sharp to the tastebuds. Sometime around the 1700s came the addition of tomatoes, and ketchup as we know it today was born. The terms catchup, catsup and ketchup all relate back to the original foreign borrowing of ke-tsiap, and all remain in use today.

STICKY CHICKEN KEBABS

Chunks of chicken with honey, mustard and tomato ketchup – sticky!

SERVES 4

2 tablespoons runny honey
2 tablespoons Heinz Tomato Ketchup
1 tablespoon Worcestershire sauce
1 heaped teaspoon Dijon mustard
1 tablespoon cider vinegar
Few dashes of Tabasco sauce (according to taste)
Pinch of salt and a good grind of freshly ground black
    pepper
4 skinless free-range chicken breasts

You will need 8 bamboo skewers pre-soaked in water
    to stop them blackening during cooking.

In a large shallow dish mix together the honey, ketchup, Worcestershire sauce, mustard, vinegar and Tabasco and then season with salt and pepper.

Cut the chicken breasts into cubes of approximately 3cm and add them to the bowl with the marinade mixture and keep turning them with a spoon until all the chicken is well coated. Cover with clingfilm and leave to marinate for 1 hour. (You can alternatively leave in the fridge overnight)

You can either fire up the barbie or pre-heat a griddle or skillet.

Thread all the chicken pieces equally onto the skewers, keeping as much of the delicious marinade on them as possible. Cook for 5–6 minutes turning on all sides as you go. Check that the chicken is thoroughly cooked before serving 2 kebabs arranged like crossed swords on a bed of parsley-flecked white rice.

ART IN THE BEST POSSIBLE TASTE

If you're all out of acrylic or oil, then look no further than the kitchen cupboard for the tools to rustle up your next masterpiece. That's what US artist Jason Baalman decided to do. He found fame after he uploaded a series of time-lapse videos to internet site YouTube which showed the creation of one of his 'ketchup-and-fries' portraits. Hundreds and thousands tuned in to watch Baalman's four minutes of whacky talent on show. His fast-growing celebrity landed him a spot on The Late Show with David Letterman, where he repeated the feat,

GOLDEN EGG BOAT CURRY

A rich creamy curry floating with spicy golden eggs.

SERVES 4

2 tablespoons sunflower oil
2 medium onions, roughly chopped
2 cloves garlic, diced
3 tablespoons Madras curry powder
4 tablespoons Heinz Tomato Ketchup
400g tin of chopped tomatoes
1 level tablespoon brown sugar
8 medium free-range eggs, hard-boiled, shelled and
    halved
4 tablespoons Greek yoghurt
150g frozen peas
Garam masala to sprinkle
Handful fresh coriander, roughly chopped

Heat the oil in a pan and fry the onions and garlic for about 10 minutes until soft and just browning. Remove from the heat, allow to cool a little and then blitz for 30 seconds to make a purée.

Return the purée to the pan, add the curry powder and ketchup and sizzle for a couple of minutes. (It seems quite apt to add ketchup to an oriental dish as the word originates from the Chinese for sauce.) Add the sugar, tomatoes and 200ml of water and bring the pan up to the boil. Reduce the heat and simmer, covered, for 15 minutes until you have a rich sauce. Check the seasoning and add salt and freshly milled black pepper if required.

Stir the yoghurt and peas into the curry sauce and simmer for a few minutes longer. Add the halved eggs to the pan, spoon the sauce over them to coat and keep simmering for a further 3–4 minutes.

Serve the curry sprinkled with a little garam masala and scattered with fresh coriander. Great served with saffron rice and mango chutney.

painting the stage manager whilst live on air, using ketchup for paint and french fries for paintbrushes. Baalman's other commissions have included working with yeast extract on toast for an Australian client, whilst another of his YouTube videos shows him painting with just chocolate and a spoon. Baalman has no formal art training. He's also wary of becoming pigeonholed as 'that guy who paints with food'. If his number of website views and media moments continue to increase, though, it will be a tag that's hard to shift.

YOU CAN'T EAT WITHOUT IT.

MOROCCAN FISH TAGINE

Flavours of the kasbah – with black olives, preserved lemons and snapper.

SERVES 4

1 tablespoon olive oil, plus extra for brushing
1 medium onion, chopped
4 plum tomatoes, sliced
2 tablespoons Heinz Tomato Ketchup
1 teaspoon ground cumin
1 teaspoon sweet paprika
500ml fish stock (you could use chicken or vegetable)
4 red snapper fillets (about 175g each) halved
    diagonally (mullet or sea bass are equally good)
12 black olives, pitted and halved
1 tablespoon tahini (sesame paste)
1/2 preserved lemon, finely chopped
1 tablespoon fresh flat leaf parsley, chopped
1 tablespoon fresh coriander, chopped
1 teaspoon fresh mint, chopped

Heat the oil in a large pan and fry the onion gently for 5 minutes. Add the tomatoes and cook for a few more minutes. Stir in the ketchup, cumin and paprika and then gradually add the fish stock. Turn the heat up to full for 2 minutes and then take the pan off the heat and keep warm.

Preheat the grill to high, brush the fillets with olive oil and season with salt and pepper. Grill skin side up for about 5 minutes. While the fish is cooking add the olives, tahini, preserved lemon and fresh herbs (reserving just a little of the herbs to garnish) to the sauce in the pan, stir gently and reheat. Check the seasoning.

Put the fish into four warmed soup bowls, spoon over the sauce and scatter the remaining herbs over the top. You could also serve this over steamed couscous or bulgur wheat.

BREAKFAST TOMATO & POTATO WAFFLES

Easy to make savoury potato waffles – perfect for a roast tomato passion.

SERVES 6

100g plain flour
1 rounded teaspoon baking powder
Pinch of salt
1 medium free-range egg
100ml milk mixed with 3 tablespoons Heinz Tomato
   Ketchup
3 teaspoons sunflower oil
150g cooked mashed potato
Freshly ground black pepper

Pick up a waffle iron from a good kitchen shop to make these waffles.

They can be prepared in advance and frozen. Simply defrost and grill before serving.

To make the waffle batter mix together in a bowl the sieved flour, baking powder and salt. Next add the egg and then the milk and ketchup mixture a little at a time and beat until you have a smooth batter. Now add the sunflower oil, the potato and season with pepper. Mix well together (your batter will no longer be smooth). Chill in the fridge for at least 2 hours or overnight ready for breakfast.

Heat a lightly oiled waffle iron until it just begins to smoke a little (or heat an electric waffle maker as per instructions) then spoon in about 100ml of batter mixture and close the lid. It will spread out on its own to a lovely oval shape. If you want a perfect rectangular waffle then its better to spread the mixture yourself to cover the complete base of the waffle iron. Cook each side over a medium high hob for 3 minutes turning only once so that they are golden brown and cooked through. Repeat until the mixture is used up, keeping the waffles warm.

These waffles are brilliant topped with grilled field mushrooms, a vine of cherry tomatoes, a mini full English breakfast or a pile of scrambled eggs.

THE WORLD'S LARGEST KETCHUP BOTTLE: COLLINSVILLE, ILLINOIS, USA, BUILT IN 1949 ON TOP OF A WATER TOWER AND STANDING 170 FEET TALL.

COCONUT, CHILLI & SQUASH SOUP

A thick, spicy and filling soup with flavours that will dance on your taste buds.

SERVES 4–6

2 tablespoons vegetable oil
2 shallots, peeled and sliced
2 spring onions, diced
2 cloves garlic, peeled and crushed (optional)
2cm fresh root ginger, peeled and finely diced
1 red birdseye chilli, deseeded and finely diced
500g butternut squash, peeled, deseeded and cut
   into 2cm cubes
250ml vegetable stock
1 tablespoon Thai fish sauce
3 tablespoons Heinz Tomato Ketchup
400ml tin coconut milk
Zest and juice of a lime
Handful fresh coriander

Heat the oil in a large saucepan and add the shallots, onions, garlic, ginger and chilli. Cook gently for 5–6 minutes until soft and then toss in the butternut squash and stir round for a couple of minutes.

Add the stock, fish sauce, ketchup and coconut milk and cook covered at a simmer for 30 minutes. Roughly chop the coriander, reserving a little for garnish, and add it to the soup together with the lime juice and zest.

Remove from the heat and allow the mixture to cool enough to blitz into a smooth soup. Reheat when ready to serve and garnish with the remaining coriander.

MARILYN, ELVIS & HEINZ

In the mid-1960s, Andy Warhol started on a series of sculptures that transformed ordinary objects into art. He employed carpenters to construct plywood boxes onto which he painted the logos of different consumer products, making them identical to supermarket cartons. When Heinz Tomato Ketchup was immortalized in such a way it took its place in the Pop Art Pantheon alongside Warhol's other 20th-century icons such as Elvis Presley and Marilyn Monroe.

CAULIFLOWER FRITTERS WITH SWEET CHILLI DIP

Delicate florets dipped in cumin batter served
with a perfectly sweet dip.

SERVES 4

For the fritters
400g squeaky fresh cauliflower, broken into bite-sized
   florets
100g gram flour (chick pea flour)
50g rice flour
$1/4$ teaspoon baking powder
Pinch cumin seeds
$1/2$ teaspoon curry powder
Vegetable oil for deep-frying

For the dip
4 tablespoons thick natural yoghurt
1 teaspoon ready-made mint sauce
1 tablespoon Heinz Tomato Ketchup
$1/2$ teaspoon lemon juice
$1/2$ red chilli, deseeded and very finely diced
Pinch of sugar
Salt and freshly ground black pepper

Bring a pan of salted water to the boil and lower the
cauliflower florets in. Boil for 2 minutes, drain and cool
on kitchen paper.

Make the dip by combining all the ingredients in a
suitable dish, cover and chill in the fridge.

Sieve the gram flour, rice flour and baking powder into
a bowl then add the cumin seeds and curry powder.
Gradually add enough water, about 175ml, to make a
smooth batter. Leave the batter to stand for 20 minutes.

Heat the vegetable oil to 190C ideally in a deep fat
fryer. Using a fork, spear each floret and dip it in the
batter, rolling it round to get it completely coated.
Allow any excess batter to drop off and then using a
knife, slide the floret off the fork and into the hot oil.
Fry in batches for 6-8 minutes until golden brown
moving them around once or twice in the oil with a
slotted spoon. Remove and drain on kitchen paper.

Serve the florets warm and the dip chilled for a perfect
starter or great accompaniment to curry dishes.

Rather than use colouring to make our ketchup red, Heinz just use tomatoes.

ANDALUCIAN FISH PIE

**Oodles of flaked Mediterranean fish, paprika
and peppers in an authentic crispy pastry.**

SERVES 6–8

For the pastry
500g flour
1 sachet dried yeast
2 free range eggs
100g butter, just melted
1 tablespoon oil
1 teaspoon sugar

For the filling
800g fish fillets (a mixture of red mullet, cod and sea
     bass would be ideal)
1 clove of garlic
1 tablespoon of freshly chopped parsley
2 tablespoons vegetable oil
2 large Spanish onions, peeled and chopped
100g sweet peppers, cored, deseeded and sliced
2 tablespoons Heinz Tomato Ketchup
1 teaspoon paprika
Plenty of salt and black pepper

(You could use fresh ready-made puff pastry for this
     recipe, rolled out very thin as this Spanish pie is
     traditionally served shallow. If you have the time
     though the authentic dough mixture makes it worth
     the effort.)

To prepare the dough, sieve the flour into a large bowl,
add the yeast, one egg and stir. Now add the butter, oil
and sugar and mix well. Add 100ml of water and then
knead the dough thoroughly for 5 minutes, then leave
to stand for 20 minutes.

Crush the garlic and mix together with the parsley.
Spread it out on a flat surface and press the fish fillets
into it. Gently fry with a little oil in a large frying pan,
skin side down for 3 minutes. Turn the fish over for
a further minute, take the pan off the heat and leave
aside for 5 minutes.

Drizzle a little oil into a separate pan and sauté the
onions until just beginning to brown. Add the peppers,
tomato ketchup, paprika and salt and cook for a further
3–4 minutes. Leave the pan and contents aside.

Preheat the oven to 180C/350F/Gas 4. Grease a 30cm
shallow round baking dish. Halve the dough and roll
out to fit the base. Spread half of the onion mixture
onto the pastry, followed by the flaked fish fillets.
Finally cover the fish with the rest of the onion mixture.
Roll out the other half of the pastry and lay on top,
pressing the edges together with the prongs of a fork
to seal. Brush with beaten egg yolk and prick the
surface 3 or 4 times with the fork. Bake in the centre
of the oven for 30 minutes until golden and crispy.
Allow to cool a little before serving.

GREEK LAMB PASTIES WITH FRESH OREGANO

Diced lamb, onions, garlic and oregano encased in shimmering filo pastry.

SERVES 4–6

1 medium onion, peeled and diced
Olive oil
200g potatoes, peeled and diced quite small
1 clove garlic, finely diced
250g lamb trimmed of excess fat and diced in
  1cm cubes
1 plum tomato, skinned and diced
2 tablespoons Heinz Tomato Ketchup
50g Feta cheese, cut into small cubes
Ready-made filo pastry
50g melted butter for brushing
Freshly ground black pepper
Handful fresh oregano

Preheat the oven to 180C/350F/Gas 4. Fry the onions in a little olive oil then add the potatoes and garlic and continue cooking for 2–3 minutes until the potatoes are just golden. Add the lamb, tomatoes and ketchup and keeping the mixture moving in the pan cook for 10 minutes. Season with black pepper. Turn up the heat for a few minutes until the liquid has evaporated and you have a dryish mixture to fill the parcels.

When using filo pastry it is important not to let it dry out so while you are working with the sheets keep the remainder under a clean, damp tea towel. Take 2 sheets, brush with melted butter and lay a third sheet on the top. Now cut the pastry into 15cm squares putting a tablespoon of the lamb mixture (approximately 75g), a cube of Feta, and a few leaves of oregano into the centre of each. Pick up one corner of the filo square and fold it in across the centre. Then fold in the opposite corner, brush with butter to make it seal. Fold in the remaining 2 corners, pinching it at the fold and butter again to completely seal the parcel. Turn the parcel over and place on the baking tray so that the joins are underneath. Repeat until all the meat mixture is used up and brush the top of each parcel with melted butter.

Cover the baking tray with foil and put in the oven. Bake for 1 hour, removing the foil for the last 10 minutes to make the pastry golden brown. Allow to cool a little before serving with a good Greek salad or with minty yoghurt on the side to make a great starter.

SMOKY JOE'S TOMATO CHUTNEY

A simple tomato chutney packed with infused smoky barbecue flavours.

MAKES ABOUT 3 x 450G JARS

2 rounded teaspoons black mustard seeds
2 rounded teaspoons coriander seeds
100g sunblush tomatoes
1kg ripe tomatoes, quartered
4 tablespoons Heinz Tomato Ketchup
2 large onions, peeled and quartered
1 dessertspoon sweet smoked paprika
1 tablespoon paprika
100g Demerara sugar
250ml sherry vinegar
1 teaspoon salt

Heat a dry heavy based frying pan and roast the mustard and coriander seeds for 2 minutes until they just begin to crackle. Remove from the heat and gently crush them in a pestle and mortar to release their flavours.

Drain the sunblush tomatoes of any oil and pat dry with kitchen paper. Place them in a food processor and blitz for a few seconds until they are roughly chopped – you do not want a smooth paste. Then add the fresh tomatoes and tomato ketchup and blitz again until they are also roughly chopped.

Transfer the tomato mixture into a large heavy based pan (or preserving pan if you have one). Next process the onions until roughly chopped like the tomatoes and add them to the pan. Add all the remaining ingredients and bring the whole mixture to the boil, stirring constantly. Reduce the heat to the lowest setting and leave to cook very gently for $2^1/_2$–3 hours. Keep an occasional eye on it and stir from time to time so that it doesn't stick.

The chutney is ready when it has absorbed all the liquid and become fairly thick.Remove the pan from the heat and allow to cool a little.

Sterilize some jars in a hot oven for 5 minutes and fill them with the chutney while still hot. Cover each with a waxed disc and seal with the lid. Allow to cool completely, label and date your Smoky Joe's Tomato Chutney and store in a cool, dry cupboard for 6–8 weeks – if you can wait that long!

YOU and HEINZ⁵⁷

together put 2¼ lb of tomatoes on the table to enjoy at every meal !

IT TAKES 2¼ lb. OF TOMATOES to make one 12-oz. bottle of Heinz Tomato Ketchup. Not just ordinary tomatoes, either! They've got to have a full-bodied flavour, a rich, red colour, plenty of juice and almost no seeds.

The tomatoes Heinz use are grown specially for them in Italy and ripened naturally in the warm Mediterranean sunshine. And, apart from a little sugar, matured vinegar and spices, nothing but the pure, whole goodness of 2¼ lb. of tomatoes goes into Heinz Tomato Ketchup. 1/4 or 2/-.

P.S. Don't forget there's Heinz Tomato Chutney too

It's delicious 2/3 or 3/- a bottle

RED THAI DUCK CURRY

Hot and spicy Thai duck with tongue-tingling fresh oriental flavours.

SERVES 4

400ml tin coconut milk
1 rounded tablespoon red Thai curry paste
2 red chillies, deseeded and sliced
2 tablespoons Heinz Tomato Ketchup
1 whole duck, pre-cooked on a rack for 1$\frac{1}{2}$ hours at
    180C/350F/Gas 4
12 cherry tomatoes, halved
Small handful torn basil leaves
2 kaffir lime leaves, chopped
1 dessertspoon Thai fish sauce

Take the whole cooked duck and remove all the meat with the skin and cut into 1cm slices.

Heat half of the tin of coconut milk in a wok or saucepan and add the chilli, red curry paste and allow to bubble for 2–3 minutes over a medium heat. Now add the rest of the coconut milk and the ketchup, bring to the boil and then simmer for 5 minutes.

Add to the wok the duck and the halved tomatoes and bring back up to the boil, reduce to a simmer adding the basil, lime leaves, sugar and fish sauce. Cook for a further 8–10 minutes and serve with fluffy rice or noodles.

PAINTING THE TOWN RED

In the 19th century days of vaudeville variety theatres, 'rotten tomatoes' were the clichéd missile of choice, pelting those stage performers deemed to be particularly bad. Into the 20th century and tomato hurling was being carried out on a far larger scale in the small Spanish town of Buñol – the scene of the world's biggest food fight. La Tomatina is acted out each August in honour of Buñol's patron saint. It's a two-hour-125,000-kilo-tomato-throwing-fest which tourists flock to.

WILD MUSHROOM DIABLO

Mixed wild mushrooms, sautéed in a fiery, creamy sauce.

SERVES 2

200g mixed fresh wild and field mushrooms
2 tablespoons Heinz Tomato Ketchup
Dash of soy sauce, about $1/4$ teaspoon
1 level teaspoon English mustard powder
Good pinch cayenne pepper
25g butter
6 tablespoons double cream or crème fraîche
1 dessertspoon fresh chopped parsley to garnish

Firstly clean the mushrooms. Do not wash them, just remove any specs of soil with a damp cloth, trim the stalks and break up any larger mushrooms.

In a small bowl mix together the ketchup, soy, mustard and cayenne. Heat the butter in a frying pan. When it just begins to foam add the mushrooms and sauté gently for 5 minutes.

Reduce the heat a little, stir in the ketchup mixture to the mushrooms and cook for 1 minute. Add the cream and continue cooking for a further couple of minutes. Taste the sauce – you can add more cayenne if you wish because 'some like it hot!'

Pour the delicious mushrooms into warmed soup bowls and serve with a flourish of parsley and wedges of warm crusty bread for dunking.

SHAKE. WAIT. SPLODGE.

Shake, shake the ketchup bottle / First none'll come, and then a lot'll. **This charming little couplet was the work of US humorist Richard Willard Armour. It was inspired, however, by fellow countryman and humorist Ogden Nash who had, some years earlier and rather more succinctly, written:** *The Catsup Bottle / First a little / Then a lottle.* **Of course, today, Nash and Armour would have had the choice of shaking and waiting or squeezing for instant ketchup gratification.**

LAMB & MINT BRUNCH BURGERS WITH RIVERSIDE SALSA

Perfect homemade burgers teased with fresh mint.

FOR 4 PEOPLE

650g minced lamb
1 large onion, grated
1 heaped teaspoon Dijon mustard
1 heaped teaspoon good quality mint sauce
$1/4$ teaspoon celery salt
Freshly ground black pepper
$1/2$ teaspoon anchovy essence
2 tablespoons Heinz Tomato Ketchup
Lea & Perrins Worcestershire sauce
1 large free-range egg, lightly whisked
1 tablespoon plain flour

Riverside Salsa
1 medium onion, peeled and finely diced
$1/3$ cucumber, peeled and finely diced
$1/2$ green apple, peeled, cored and finely diced
2 teaspoons lime juice
2 teaspoons mango chutney, cutting up any large lumps
1 heaped tablespoon fresh chopped coriander leaves
$1/2$ teaspoon roasted cumin seeds
1 teaspoon sweet tamarind sauce
2 tablespoons Heinz Tomato Ketchup

For the salsa. In a bowl mix the onion, cucumber and apple, add the lime juice (to stop the apple browning) and toss together. In a separate bowl mix together the remaining salsa ingredients and then combine everything together and you are ready to go. This is a really fresh tasting salsa but it will only last a day in the fridge.

Scrunch up and separate the minced lamb and place in a large bowl, add the onion, Dijon mustard, mint sauce, tomato ketchup, anchovy essence, celery salt, pepper and a good splash of Worcestershire sauce and mix all these together well using your hands or a wooden spoon. Now add the whisked egg and sprinkle the flour evenly mixing all the ingredients together well. Divide the mixture into 4 equal portions and using your hands mould into patties about 1.5cm thick. Place on greaseproof paper and refrigerate for 1 hour or until you are ready to cook them.

Heat a griddle or heavy based frying pan with a little sunflower oil and when hot cook the burgers over a medium to high heat. This should take no longer than 8 minutes, turning once. As it is lamb don't overcook it – they are better if still a little pink in the middle but golden on the outside. Remove and serve on warmed sesame seed baps topped with the Riverside Salsa.

The long and the short of it is...
no other ketchup tastes like Heinz

There's a new shape in Heinz Tomato Ketchup bottles–a 12-oz. bottle with a wider, easier-pouring neck. But whether you buy it in the new shape or the old shape it's still the same Heinz Tomato Ketchup. The ketchup that tastes different.

It tastes different because we make it different. We don't use artificial flavouring, preservatives, artificial colouring, or thickeners. We use nothing but natural ingredients in Heinz Tomato Ketchup – ripe tomatoes (over a pound and a half in every 12-oz. bottle), homely spices, and Heinz know-how. That's the difference.

And that's why, in any shape or form, no other ketchup tastes like Heinz.

LET'S HEAR IT FOR BANGERS.

A PAT ON THE BACK FOR THE HOT DOG.

TK & PASSIONFRUIT ICE-CREAM

Divine on its own or as a perfect accompaniment to a mixed seafood or smoked fish salad or antipasto.

MAKES 2 LITRES

8 egg yolks
150g caster sugar
125g fresh passionfruit pulp (or 4–6 passionfruit)
125g fresh tomato pulp
4 tablespoons Heinz Tomato Ketchup
2 tablespoons lemon juice
300ml double cream

Put the egg yolks and caster sugar into a food processor and blend until they turn a pale creamy colour. Add the passionfruit, tomatoes, ketchup and lemon juice and blitz again for about 30 seconds.

In a separate large bowl whip the cream until it forms stiff peaks. Pour in the blended mixture and fold in the cream with a plastic spatula until it is well combined. Put into a plastic tub and freeze for about 45 minutes. (If you have a fast freeze facility then this will only take about 20 minutes.)

Remove from the freezer and stir the ice cream well. Return to the freezer for 45 minutes (or 20 minutes) remove and repeat the stirring. This will avoid the ice cream crystallising. You may need to do this one further time just before the ice cream is completely frozen.

Flavours can be blunted by the cold so leave the ice-cream to stand at room temperature for a few minutes before serving decorated with a stem of fresh redcurrants and some dark chocolate shavings.

PASTRAMI, ROCKET & RED CHARD SALAD WITH RYE CROUTONS

Sumptuous starter with big flavour and a thick herb and tomato dressing.

SERVES 4

For the tomato and ginger vinaigrette
1 large vine ripened tomato, peeled and de-seeded
(cover the tomato with boiling water for one minute,
lift it out and the skin will come off easily)
1 level teaspoon fresh ginger, grated
2 tablespoons of Heinz Tomato Ketchup
2 tablespoons olive oil
3 teaspoons balsamic vinegar
2 teaspoons red wine vinegar
Freshly ground black pepper
Salt

2 handfuls of rocket leaves
1 handful of red chard leaves
1 handful of baby lettuce leaves
1 red onion, sliced into slithers
300g pastrami, thinly sliced
2 slices rye bread
Sea salt
Olive oil

To make the vinaigrette place all the ingredients in a blender except the olive oil and the salt. Blitz together adding the olive oil in a steady stream until you have a thick and delicious sauce. Now add a pinch or two of salt and taste. (Top tip – if you add the salt earlier it may stop the mixture emulsifying.) This vinaigrette will keep for several days in the fridge but be sure to bring back to room temperature before serving.

Remove the crusts and then cut the rye bread into cubes of about 1.5cm. Spread them on a baking sheet, sprinkle with a good pinch of sea salt and drizzle with olive oil. Put into a medium hot oven for about 10 minutes until golden. Remove and keep on kitchen paper.

Put the salad leaves and onion together in a large bowl, spoon over the dressing and toss the leaves. Divide the salad between 4 plates, arrange strips of pastrami over the top and scatter with the rye croûtons.

Now Mrs. Beeton gets together with Heinz to cook with ketchup

It's the new, exciting way to add that touch of variety to your meals. Rich, red Heinz Tomato Ketchup in the cooking makes a delicious change in your favourite dishes!

We've taken some of the famous recipes from the 1961 Mrs. Beeton's Cookery Book. But we've added Heinz Tomato Ketchup. And presto! The same delicious meal—but with a difference.

Here, for a fascinating change, is Mrs. Beeton's Chicken in Casserole... with Heinz Tomato Ketchup. It's an easy treat to give your family, so why not make it tonight?

A REFRIGERATOR A DAY TO BE WON DURING SEPTEMBER
in the new "Cook with Ketchup" competition! And there are more delicious recipes, too. Entry forms from your local Heinz stockist.

HEINZ 57 Tomato Ketchup

CHICKEN IN CASSEROLE

1 chicken	1 shallot
1 oz. flour	2 oz. chopped mushrooms
Salt and pepper	1 pint stock
2 oz. butter or dripping	2 tablespoons
4-6 oz. streaky bacon	Heinz Tomato Ketchup

Joint the chicken, dip joints in flour and seasoning. Melt the fat in a casserole; fry the bacon, cut in strips; add chicken, mushrooms and chopped shallot. Fry until golden brown, turning when necessary. Add hot stock, sufficient just to cover the chicken, simmer until tender . . . about 1½ hours. Add 2 tablespoons of Heinz Tomato Ketchup, bring to the boil, and correct the seasoning.

Serve in the casserole. 6 helpings.

BANGERS & MASH WITH A RED ONION GRAVY

Always a popular family dish but with added zingy red onion gravy.

SERVES 2

1 medium red onion
Olive oil
1 teaspoon fresh thyme leaves
Salt and freshly ground black pepper
500g potatoes (Maris Piper or a similar floury potato
    would be good)
4–6 proper butchers' handmade sausages
Knob of butter
300ml good beef stock
100ml red wine (if the cook can spare it!)
1 tablespoon Heinz Tomato Ketchup
1 rounded teaspoon Dijon mustard

Cut the onion in half and then each half into four segments and put them into a small roasting dish, drizzle with olive oil, sprinkle the thyme over and season with salt and pepper. Roast in a medium-hot oven for 20 minutes.

Peel the potatoes and cut into chunks. Boil in lightly salted water for 15–20 minutes until cooked through. Grill the sausages gently under a medium heat, turning as needed for 15–20 minutes.

In the meantime make the onion gravy. Bring the stock up to the boil in a pan and add the red wine and ketchup. Turn down the heat a little and reduce the liquid by half to thicken it, which takes about 10 minutes. Take the roasted onions out of the oven and add them to the gravy halfway through the cooking time, pressing them down with a fork to release the segments.

Drain the cooked potatoes, add a knob of butter, a splash of milk, the Dijon mustard, season with black pepper and mash well. At this stage you can use your ricer to make perfect creamy mashed potato or using a fairly open mesh sieve press the potato through with a wooden spoon to gain the same sumptuous effect. (If you don't fancy mustard try adding horseradish or chopped watercress.)

To serve this great traditional dish, place a good dollop of mash on the plate, push the sausages into the mash at jaunty angles and pour over the rich onion gravy.

CHARGRILLED BRILL WITH TOMATO & DILL BUTTER

Chunky sea brill, seared and served with provocative dill and tomato aromas.

SERVES 2

4 tablespoons unsalted butter, softened
1 tablespoon Heinz Tomato Ketchup
1 teaspoon chopped fresh dill
2 brill fillets (around 225g each)
Olive oil
Sea salt
Dill fronds to garnish

Mash together the butter, ketchup and dill and chill in the fridge for 10 minutes. Remove, scoop out onto clingfilm and roll into a fat sausage about 6cm long by 3cm diameter. Seal it up and freeze for 1 hour.

Brush the fish fillets with olive oil and season with salt. Cook them on a hot ridged griddle, skin side up for 2 minutes turn and repeat for a further 3–4 depending on the thickness of the fillets. Remove the pan from the heat leaving the fillets in the pan for 1 minute more.

Take the tomato butter from the freezer, leave to stand for a couple of minutes and slice off rounds less than 1cm thick. Place the brill fillets on warm serving plates and lay 3 slices of tomato butter down each fillet, topped with a frond of dill. This is a delicious dish to serve with some crunchy stir-fry vegetables like mange-tout, baby corn, bean sprouts or broccoli.

PULP-TASTIC KETCHUP

Quentin Tarantino obviously has a penchant for ketchup – he managed to squeeze two references to the glorious red stuff into his film, *Pulp Fiction*. First, an exchange between his two hitmen characters, exploring the differences between American and Dutch consumer cultures: Vincent: *'You know what they put on French fries in Holland instead of ketchup?'* Jules: *What?* Vincent: *'Mayonnaise.'* Jules: *Goddamn.* Vincent: *I've seen 'em do it, man. And I don't mean a little bit on the side of the plate...'*

TK PARMESAN STRAWS

Cheesy twists of flaky pastry – perfect dippers.

MAKES AROUND 20 CHEESE STRAWS

150g grated Parmesan
454g chilled fresh puff pastry
4 tablespoons Heinz Tomato Ketchup

Preheat the oven to 220C/425F/Gas 7. Scatter your work surface with half the Parmesan, place the pastry on top and cut it in half. Roll out the halves until the pastry is about 1cm thick and then spread all over with the ketchup. Sprinkle with the remaining Parmesan and fold the pastry sheets over to sandwich the ketchup and roll out again to about 1cm thick.

Lay some baking parchment onto 2 large baking trays. Cut the pastry widthways into 1cm strips and taking each strip by the ends rotate into a tight rope twist and lay on the baking sheets pressing the ends down onto the tray to secure them. Continue until you have used all the pastry. Chill in the fridge for 20 minutes and then put straight into the hot oven. Bake for 10–15 minutes until golden all over. Cool a little on a rack and then serve while still warm.

Then, there's a joke and a promise that it won't be funny:
'Three tomatoes are walking down the street – a poppa tomato, a momma tomato, and a little baby tomato. Baby tomato starts lagging behind. Poppa tomato gets angry, goes over to the baby tomato, and squishes him... and says, 'Ketchup'. Most, of course, would claim that Tarantino's real love of ketchup is all too evident in his films: it's usually spattered by the litre-load across his characters as each meet their gruesome ends!

GAZPACHO WITH ANCHOVY CROUTON

A chilled explosion of fresh vegetable tastes and salty toasts.

SERVES 6

900g ripe vine tomatoes
2 cloves of garlic, crushed
50g fresh white breadcrumbs
2 tablespoons red wine vinegar
3 tablespoons extra virgin olive oil
900g ripe vine tomatoes
$\frac{1}{2}$ cucumber, peeled, deseeded and chopped
2 spring onions, thinly sliced
1 red pepper, deseeded and finely chopped
1 yellow pepper, deseeded and finely chopped
1 tablespoon chopped fresh flat leaf parsley
1 tablespoon torn basil leaves
250ml iced water
2 tablespoons Heinz Tomato Ketchup
$\frac{1}{2}$ teaspoon celery salt and freshly ground black pepper
Handful of ice cubes

For the croûtons
10 anchovy fillets
Small knob of butter
4 thick slices stale bread, crusts removed
Olive oil

Peel and deseed the tomatoes – the easy way is to pour boiling water over them in a bowl and leave for a minute then the skins will fall away from the flesh. Put all the ingredients, except the salt, pepper and ice cubes, into a blender and blitz until puréed. Now add the celery salt and pepper to taste. (Bear in mind that you are going to be adding anchovy croûtons, which are salty). Pour the soup into a large bowl, cover and chill.

Preheat the oven to medium high. Lay the anchovies in a small frying pan and sauté with the butter – you will find that they almost dissolve. Spread the anchovy butter all over the bread and cut into 1.5cm cubes. Scatter the cubes on a tray and bake in the oven for about 5 minutes and then flip them over. Keep an eye on them, as they will turn colour very suddenly. Allow to cool.

To serve, pour the chilled gazpacho into soup bowls, add a couple of ice cubes to each dish and then scatter the croûtons over the gazpacho.

IT'S RED MAGIC TIME!

It's only natural...

You won't find anything artificial about Heinz Tomato Ketchup. No artificial thickeners. No artificial preservatives. No artificial colouring. No artificial flavour. They just don't grow in Heinz ketchup bottles.

It's only good natural ingredients you'll find there. A few homely spices and a whole lot of tomatoes. In fact, we use a pound and a half of good ripe tomatoes to make just three-quarters of a pound of thick, rich Heinz ketchup.

You can't improve on nature, we reckon.

No other ketchup tastes like Heinz

IT'S ONLY NATURAL...

GOULASH WITH HORSERADISH & HERB DUMPLINGS

Strips of beef in a rich tomato sauce with fluffy dumplings.

SERVES 4

For the goulash
1kg diced braising steak
2 tablespoons plain flour
Salt and freshly milled black pepper
25g butter
1 tablespoon sunflower oil
2 large onions, peeled and chopped
1 red pepper, deseeded and sliced
2 tablespoons Heinz Tomato Ketchup
1 tablespoon paprika
600ml good beef stock
140ml tub of soured cream
Handful fresh chives, snipped

For the dumplings
125g self-raising flour
Good pinch of salt
50g suet
2 rounded teaspoons horseradish sauce
$\frac{1}{2}$ teaspoon freshly chopped parsley
$\frac{1}{2}$ teaspoon freshly chopped oregano
$\frac{1}{2}$ teaspoon freshly chopped thyme
$\frac{1}{2}$ teaspoon freshly chopped chives
(If you don't have the fresh herbs you can use
    1 heaped teaspoon of dried mixed herbs)

Preheat the oven to 150C/300F/Gas 2. Put the beef into a large bowl and sieve the flour over it, add salt and pepper and toss to coat each piece of meat. Heat the butter and oil in a large heavy based frying pan and brown the beef in batches, separating the chunks of meat as they cook. Using a slotted spoon transfer the meat to a casserole dish wide enough to accommodate the dumplings later.

Add the onions to the same pan and fry for 5–6 minutes until soft. Add the pepper and cook for a further few minutes and transfer to the casserole. Back to the pan, add the ketchup, paprika and stock and bring it all to the boil scraping the base to deglaze the pan, gathering up the good flavoured bits. Pour the mixture over the beef in the casserole, stir, cover and cook in the oven for $1\frac{1}{2}$ hours until the beef is tender.

While the beef is cooking you can prepare the dumplings. Sieve the flour and salt into a bowl and add the suet, horseradish and herbs and mix well. Add enough water (4–5 tablespoons) to make a firm but pliable dough. Using floured hands, form into 8 golf ball sized dumplings.

Remove the casserole from the oven and turn the temperature up to 180C/350F/Gas 6. Drop the dumplings into the casserole where they will settle on top of the goulash. Replace the lid and return it to the oven for 15 minutes until the dumplings are puffy and fluffy.

Lift out the dumplings with a slotted spoon and put them on warm serving plates. Stir the soured cream into the goulash and spoon onto the plates and garnish with the chopped chives.

CHORIZO & SUMMER VEGETABLE OMELETTE

A regional Spanish omelette served hot or cold – a summer spectacular.

SERVES 4–6

3 tablespoons olive oil
1 Spanish onion, sliced
salt and black pepper
450g waxy potatoes, peeled, cut into ½cm slices, rinsed and dried
6 large eggs
Handful broad beans, blanched
Handful frozen peas, defrosted
2 tomatoes, sliced
50g chorizo, thinly sliced

Heat 1 tablespoon of oil in a large deep non-stick frying pan; add the onions and fry gently for 6–8 minutes until soft and golden. Season well with salt and pepper. Transfer the onions into a bowl.

Using the same pan, add the rest of the olive oil and sauté half the potatoes at a time until golden. Drain the potatoes on kitchen paper and then add them to the onions.

In a separate bowl whisk the eggs and season well. Now add the eggs, beans and peas to the potatoes and onions and carefully mix together.

Preheat the grill to medium. Reheat the large frying pan and then pour in the omelette mixture. Turn down the heat and cook the omelette for 4–6 minutes until the base is set and the egg on top is still runny. Remove the pan from the heat, spoon on 4 big blobs of ketchup and marble in with a fork. Lay the sliced tomatoes and chorizo on top. Put under the grill for 4–6 minutes until the top sets and just starts to turn golden. Cut into wedges and serve hot or cold for the perfect summer lunch.

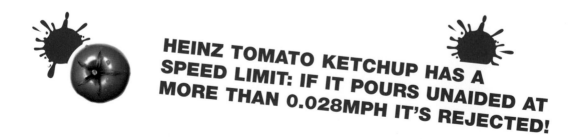

HEINZ TOMATO KETCHUP HAS A SPEED LIMIT: IF IT POURS UNAIDED AT MORE THAN 0.028MPH IT'S REJECTED!

TK FIERY BARBECUE MARINADE

Hot summer days need this sizzling summer marinade for meat or vegetables.

1 small onion, finely diced
2 birdseye chillies, deseeded and finely diced
1 tablespoon olive oil
4 tablespoons Heinz Tomato Ketchup
200ml orange juice
1 teaspoon marmalade
1 teaspoon soy sauce
1 tablespoon muscovado sugar
1 level teaspoon dry mustard powder
1 tablespoon horseradish sauce
Pinch cayenne pepper

Gently fry the onions and chillies in the olive oil for about 5 minutes. Add all the other ingredients bring to the boil and then reduce the heat and let it bubble away for 3–4 minutes to slowly infuse all the scrummy flavours.

When its cooled keep it in a small bowl or a jar and use it to marinate your barbecue meats and vegetables – it works especially well with pork, chicken and butternut squash.

BEST BUDDIES #1

THE BURGER. Ground meat was being eaten back in Egyptian times. Meat patties can be traced back to the Mongol Empire; and placing it between bread allowed armies to eat whilst they marched. Fast-forward to the 18th century, to the German town of Hamburg that gave the snack its name, patties were made of ground beef, onion and breadcrumbs. Emigrants took the burger to America; its convenience as a quick handheld snack took off and ketchup finally crowned its glory!

VEGGIE MOUSSAKA

A mêlée of Mediterranean vegetables packed with sunshine flavours.

SERVES 4

1 tablespoon olive oil
1 red onion, peeled and chopped
1 clove garlic (optional)
1 leek, cut into 1cm slices
1 red and one green pepper, deseeded and chunked
150g mushrooms, roughly chopped
400g tin of chopped tomatoes
2 tablespoons Heinz Tomato Ketchup
400g tin Cannellini beans, drained
1 teaspoon chopped fresh thyme
1 teaspoon chopped fresh oregano
1 large (or 2 small) aubergines, sliced
200g thick Greek yoghurt
50g Feta cheese, crumbled
1 large free-range egg

Preheat the oven to 180C/350F/Gas 4. Heat half the oil in a pan and sauté the onions until soft. Add the garlic and leek and cook for 3–4 minutes then add the peppers, mushrooms, tomatoes and ketchup. Cook gently for 10 minutes and then add the herbs and beans. Season with salt and freshly milled black pepper.

Heat the grill and using the remainder of the olive oil brush both sides of the aubergine slices and pop them under the grill for a few minutes on each side until golden. (Aubergines absorb a huge amount of oil if fried so it is much better to grill or dry griddle them.)

Lay half the aubergine slices on the bottom of a large shallow ovenproof dish then cover with half of the vegetable mixture. Repeat with the rest of the aubergines and top with the remaining mixture.

Whisk together the yoghurt, half the Feta cheese and the egg. Pour this over the veggie mixture and spread to cover with the back of a spoon. Sprinkle the rest of the Feta cheese over the top and season with black pepper. Bake in the hot oven for 40–50 minutes until the top is golden brown. Allow to cool slightly before serving with a crunchy Cos lettuce and watercress salad.

RIB STEAKS WITH STILTON SAUCE

Juicy steaks, perfectly seared with a blue cheese and tomato ketchup hat.

SERVES 2

100g field mushrooms, sliced
20g butter
100g Stilton
1 teaspoon runny honey
2 tablespoons Heinz Tomato Ketchup
Ground white pepper
Tablespoon fresh, snipped chives
Vegetable oil
2 rib-eye steaks

Melt the butter in a frying pan over a medium heat. When it begins to froth, slide in the mushrooms and sauté for 3–4 minutes until soft. Remove from the heat and tip the mushrooms with their buttery juices into a blender. Now crumble the Stilton into the blender along with the tomato ketchup, honey and a good pinch of white pepper. Blitz until you have a smooth paste. To finish the sauce, stir in (do not blitz) two-thirds of the chopped chives.

Heat a griddle or heavy based frying pan that has been first coated with a very small amount of vegetable oil until just beginning to smoke. Slap in the steaks and cook for 2–3 minutes on each side for medium – adjust the cooking time if you want the steaks rare or well done.

Once the steaks are cooked heat the grill to high. Now spread the rich creamy mushroom and cheese sauce thickly over the steaks and pop under the grill until the sauce just begins to bubble into brown specks – this won't take long. It is well worth resting the steaks for a couple of minutes before garnishing with the remaining chives and serving with homemade French fries.

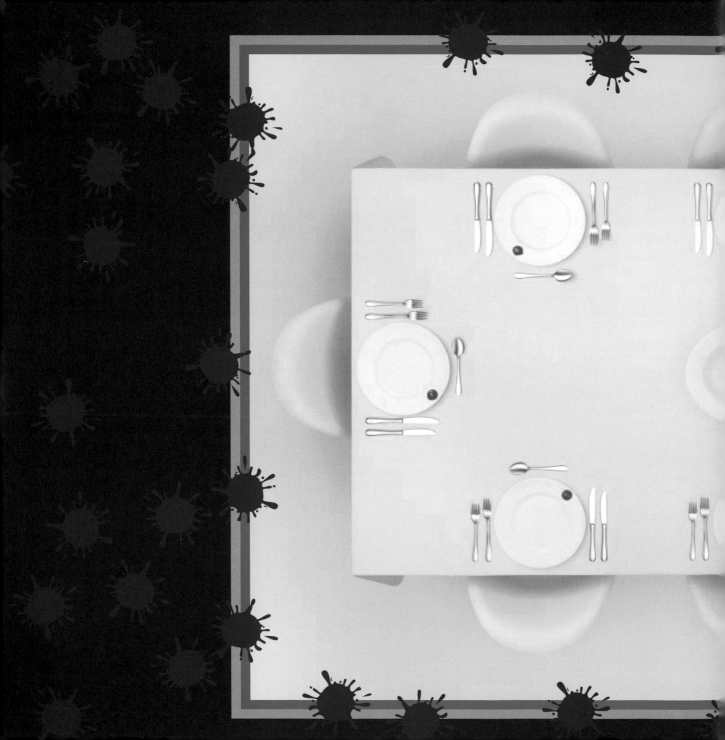

YOU CAN'T EAT WITHOUT IT.

PORK & APPLE MEATLOAF

What a great combination! Serve this as a hot starter or a cold lunch.

SERVES 6–8

1 onion, grated
1 tablespoon olive oil
500g minced pork
200g cooked white rice (about 70g uncooked)
2 green apples, peeled, cored and grated
2 medium free-range eggs, beaten
2 tablespoons Heinz Tomato Ketchup
Good splash Worcestershire sauce
Good pinch freshly grated nutmeg
1 heaped teaspoon dried mixed herbs
Salt and plenty of freshly milled black pepper

Preheat the oven to 190C/375F/Gas 5. Fry the onions in the olive oil for 3–4 minutes until soft. In a large bowl combine all the remaining ingredients, add the onions and thoroughly mix together with your hands or a wooden spoon.

Butter a 1lb loaf tin, press the mixture into it and bake in the centre of the oven uncovered for 1¼ hours. Remove from the oven, allow to cool slightly and then release from the mould. You can serve this warm or cold with a mixed salad and home made parsnip crisps. It makes a great starter, a lovely lunch and perfect fried in slices for breakfast. It will keep for 4–5 days in the fridge.

BEST BUDDIES #2

THE HOT DOG. The wienerwurst can be traced back to Vienna; the frankfurter to Frankfurt; and the 'dachshund' or 'little dog' sausage has been attributed to a 17th century Bavarian butcher. Whilst mystery and lore shroud the true etymology of the sausage, what's certain is that by the 20th century, its place as one of the most popular vendor foods was well and truly established, and no self-respecting stall owner would be without ketchup and mustard condiment bottles to the side.

ROASTED RED PEPPER SALAD

A stylish Provencal salad finished with a flourish of chargrilled red peppers.

SERVES 4–6

200ml Madeira wine
100ml red wine vinegar
1 tablespoon Heinz Tomato Ketchup
2 level dessertspoons Demerara sugar
6cm cinnamon stick
2 whole cloves
Good pinch grated nutmeg
100ml light olive oil (the cheaper basic olive oil works best)
3–4 sweet red peppers
Mixed green salad leaves
50g hard goats cheese
50g shelled walnuts, lightly crushed

Pour into a small saucepan the Madeira, vinegar, ketchup, sugar and spices and bring to the boil stirring to dissolve the sugar. Keep boiling until the liquid is reduced down by half to about 150ml. Leave to cool.

Remove and discard the cinnamon stick and cloves and transfer the remaining liquid to a blender. Gradually add the olive oil while the blender is running. You can make this vinaigrette the day before and keep in the fridge but you must bring it back to room temperature before using or you will lose some of the flavour.

Char the red peppers until just blackened all over. You can use tongs over a gas flame, a hot grill or a dry griddle pan – whichever suits you. Carefully transfer the peppers to a bowl, cover with clingfilm and leave for 10 minutes. After this time you will find you can remove the skin easily with a sharp knife, working down from the stalk, which can be discarded together with any seeds or pith from inside the pepper. Cut the peppers into strips, put into a bowl and pour the vinaigrette over them. Leave for half an hour to infuse the flavours.

Arrange the salad leaves on the plates, lift the peppers from the dressing and lay them on top. Using a potato peeler shave off peelings of goats cheese and scatter them over the salad together with the walnuts. Drizzle the vinaigrette over and around the salad and serve.

Makes a fun lunch with some warm, yielding focaccia bread or a deliciously light starter for dinner.

AT THE 1893 CHICAGO WORLD'S FAIR, MORE THAN 1,000,000 HEINZ PICKLE PINS WERE HANDED OUT: A PROMOTIONAL PHENOMENON!

FRAGRANT MARTINI MUSSELS

Delicious mussels, poached in vermouth with a fresh and aromatic twist.

SERVES 2 AS A STARTER

400g fresh mussels
1 tablespoon olive oil
2 large shallots, finely chopped
1 stalk of lemongrass, finely sliced
2 tablespoons Heinz Tomato Ketchup
175ml dry Martini
1 tablespoon fresh coriander, leaves and stems finely
   chopped
1 tablespoon flat leaf parsley, finely chopped
1 lemon (half for zest and half for serving wedges)

Put the mussels into the sink and cover with fresh cold water. Discard any mussels that are open or damaged or do not close when tapped. Scrape or scrub them clean of any barnacles and pull away any beards and then put the mussels back into clean fresh water.

Heat a large saucepan over a low heat, big enough to contain the mussels, add the olive oil, the shallots and lemongrass. Fry gently until just softened. Add the ketchup, Martini, parsley (reserving a little to garnish), coriander and lemon zest. Turn up the heat and when the liquid is bubbling add the mussels to the pan. Stir them well in the sauce and then cover and cook over a high heat for 6–8 minutes, shaking the pan quite vigorously once or twice with the lid on.

As soon as the mussels have opened transfer them to warm serving bowls with a slotted spoon, pour the sauce all over and scatter with the remaining parsley. Serve with lemon wedges and lots of crusty bread for dunking in the sauce.

SHERRIED DUCK WITH WATERCRESS MASH

Quacking lovely Gressingham duck marinated and sautéed in sherry.

SERVES 4

Vegetable oil
1 red onion, diced
1 carrot, peeled and cut into julienne matchsticks
1 teaspoon fresh chopped parsley
1 teaspoon fresh chopped thyme
2 bay leaves
2 vine tomatoes, chopped
2 tablespoons Heinz Tomato Ketchup
4 free-range Gressingham duck breasts (175–200g each)
175ml sweet sherry
Sea salt and black pepper

For the mash
500g potatoes (King Edwards or Maris Piper) peeled
    and cut up
Knob of butter
Salt and freshly milled black pepper
40g fresh watercress, roughly chopped

Put a tablespoon of oil into a large frying pan and add the onion, carrot and herbs. Cook gently for 6–8 minutes until the carrot has softened then add the tomatoes and ketchup, season with salt and pepper, remove from the heat and keep aside.

Boil the potatoes in salted water until cooked through. Drain and mash with a splash of milk and a knob of butter. Cover and keep warm.

Heat a heavy based frying pan, add no oil as the duck will produce its own fat, and when hot place the duck breasts skin side down to sear them. Cook for 5 minutes, turn over and leave for a further 3–4 minutes.

At this point transfer the duck breasts to the pan with the carrot mix and nestle them in amongst it. Set the pan back over a high heat and add the sherry. Once bubbling, reduce the heat and simmer for 5 minutes until the sauce has thickened.

Stir the watercress into the mashed potato. Re-heat for a couple of minutes if necessary. Carefully lift out the duck breasts onto a board and cut each one diagonally into 1cm slices. Using a fish slice lift each duck portion onto a hot plate, press down lightly to fan it out and now spoon over the sauce. Add a good dollop of watercress mash and serve.

There's more to Heinz than meets the eye

Over 2 lb. of pampered, perfect tomatoes go into every 15-oz. bottle of Heinz Tomato Ketchup.

Tomatoes highlighted with a hint of spice and vinegar and subtly improved with a touch of seasoning.

But there's another touch which is even more important. The Heinz touch.

It's a matter of balance and blending, of care and cooking. Combined with the finest ingredients it makes the ketchup with the best-loved flavour in the world.

You can't see the Heinz touch. But you can taste it. Ask your family.

No other ketchup has the Heinz touch

52

BALSAMIC BARBECUE RIBS

Classic pork spare ribs with a sweet sensation in the marinade.

SERVES 4–6

2kg pork spare ribs – if you ask your butcher he
   will prepare these for you

For the sauce
1 onion, finely diced
Olive oil
1 x 500g carton Heinz Creamed Tomatoes
75g dark muscovado sugar
75ml balsamic vinegar
Juice of half a lime
4 tablespoons Heinz Tomato Ketchup
1 level teaspoon chilli powder
2 tablespoons dark rum or bourbon

Pre-heat the oven to 200C/400F/Gas 6. Lay the ribs out in a single layer on a rack over a large roasting tin and roast for 30 minutes. It is important to use a rack to allow the fat to drain.

While the ribs are roasting you can make the sauce. Sweat the onions with a drizzle of olive oil in a saucepan until just translucent, but not browned. Now add all the other sauce ingredients to the pan, turn up the heat and when it starts to bubble reduce and simmer for 10 minutes.

Remove the ribs from the oven and carefully drain off the fat in the roasting tin. Tip the ribs from the rack back into the roasting tin and pour the sauce over them making sure they are well coated.

Reduce the oven temperature to 180C/350F/Gas 4 and cook the ribs for a further 1–1$\frac{1}{4}$ hours until tender, turning the ribs in the sauce from time to time.

(If you are planning a barbecue you can cook these in advance and give them a last sizzle over the hot coals.)

PORK SWEET & SOUR

A real oriental favourite with a fabulous homemade sweet and sour sauce

SERVES 2

450g lean belly pork (cut into 1.5cm cubes)
2 tablespoons sesame oil
1 spring onion, finely chopped
2 teaspoons root ginger, finely chopped
1 clove garlic, finely diced
1 tablespoon light soy sauce
2 tablespoons white sugar
3 tablespoons white wine vinegar
2 tablespoons Heinz Tomato Ketchup
4 tablespoons water
Pineapple, to serve

Heat the oil in a wok and then fry the pork until the traces of fat are just golden and crispy, about 4–5 minutes, ensuring that the meat is cooked through. Remove from the pan with a slotted spoon and drain on kitchen paper.

Pour out any excess oil leaving a coating in the wok and add the spring onion, ginger and garlic and stir-fry for a couple of minutes. Add the sugar, soy, vinegar, ketchup and water and bring to the boil. Turn down the heat and allow the sauce to reduce and thicken slightly.

Return the pork to the wok and stir it in the hot sauce for 2 minutes. Serve over noodles or rice with chunks of griddled pineapple.

A TIGHT SQUEEZE!

Heinz pack a staggering 126g of ripe, fresh tomatoes into every 100g of tomato ketchup that they make. That's a tight fit! And to keep ketchup lovers happy with enough of their favourite red condiment, Heinz uses a quantity of fresh tomatoes sufficient to fill an Olympic-size swimming pool – every day of the year. It guarantees a great taste but it also means it's a potent source of the powerful antioxidant lycopene.

SPINACH, PEPPER AND MUSHROOM TERRINE

Stunning layers of vibrant colours of rosy red and vibrant green.

SERVES 6–8

1kg sweet red peppers, skinned and deseeded
2 tablespoons Heinz Tomato Ketchup
50g stale breadcrumbs
4 egg whites
Olive oil
450g chestnut mushrooms, sliced
1 teaspoon chopped fresh basil
1 teaspoon chopped fresh oregano (or good pinch of dried)
Sea salt and freshly ground black pepper
350g fresh spinach leaves, stalks removed

To skin the peppers place them under a hot grill and scorch them all over. Transfer them to a paper bag and seal it up. After a few minutes you will be able to remove the skins quite easily with a small knife. Put the skinned peppers in a blender together with the ketchup, half the breadcrumbs and half the egg whites and blend thoroughly. Transfer the mixture to a bowl and keep cool.

Cook the chestnut mushrooms gently in a frying pan with a little olive oil for 5 minutes then increase the heat, stirring often, and cook for 10 minutes more until all the moisture has evaporated. Allow to cool a little and then in a clean jug blitz the mushrooms together with the remaining breadcrumbs and egg whites until you have a good smooth mixture. Add the herbs, season with salt and pepper and blitz very briefly. Set aside and keep cool.

Preheat the oven to 200C/400F/Gas 6. Blanch the spinach for 1 minute in a large pan of boiling water then drain and press out as much moisture as possible on kitchen paper. Line a 1lb terrine with baking parchment and spoon in half the sweet pepper purée. Lay half of the spinach all over and then add all the mushroom mixture followed by the rest of the spinach and finally the remaining sweet pepper mixture. Cover with baking parchment and bake in the oven for one hour.

Leave to cool in the tin for a few hours and then turn out onto a serving plate.

TOMATO-CRUSTED LAMB RACK WITH BABY VEGETABLES

A Guard of Honour wearing a crunchy tomato coat.

SERVES 2

2 racks of lamb (about 3 bones per person)
2 tablespoons Heinz Tomato Ketchup
1 tablespoon chopped fresh mint
1 tablespoon chopped fresh flat leaf parsley
1 whole spring onion, finely chopped
8 baby courgettes
8 baby carrots
8 baby new potatoes
10 green olives, pitted and halved
Zest of $\frac{1}{2}$ a lemon
Olive oil
Sea salt and freshly ground black pepper

(This recipe uses baby courgettes and baby carrots but
  any baby vegetables in season would be good.)

Preheat the oven to 200C/400F/Gas 6. Pat the fat
side of the lamb with kitchen paper to thoroughly dry.
Score the lamb rack in both directions making diamond
shapes in the fat (much like you would to make pork
crackling). Spread it with tomato ketchup and push
into the slits with a knife. Mix together the mint,
parsley, spring onion and press the mixture over the
tomato ketchup. Place the lamb herb side up in a
roasting pan and cook for 10 minutes.

Remove the pan from the oven and add the potatoes,
courgettes and carrots topped with the olives and
lemon zest, drizzle with olive oil and season with salt
and pepper. Return the pan to the oven and cook the
vegetables with the lamb for a further 25 minutes.
This will cook the lamb to pink, so add 5–15 minutes
if you like it more well done.

Remove the pan from the oven and allow the lamb
to rest for 5 minutes, keeping the vegetables warm.
Arrange the vegetables neatly on warm serving plates
adding the lamb which you have sliced into cutlets.

KETCHUP CAN BE FOUND IN THE KITCHENS OF 97% OF AMERICAN HOMES!

No one grows Ketchup like Heinz.

No one
grows
Ketchup
like

THE TOMATO KETCHUP YEARS...

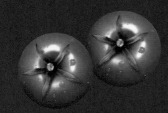

A LITTLE HEINZ HISTORY

1844 Henry John Heinz is born in a small American village outside Pittsburgh.

1869 Henry J. Heinz founds the company. The first product is horseradish, presented in clear glass bottles. Competitors chose to conceal the contents of their jars behind green glass. By opting for transparency, the quality of Heinz' product was clear for all to see.

1876 Heinz launches Tomato Ketchup as part of his range. The ketchup was intended as a convenience food, as a 'blessed relief for mother and other women in the household', since making ketchup in those days was an arduous and messy affair.

1882 Heinz patents the design of his glass ketchup bottle.

1890 The brand identity comes together, with the development of the keystone logo. Also, the screw cap is introduced.

1898 Heinz proudly announces that there is no condiment more universally popular than ketchup.

1905 Heinz are producing more than 5 million bottles worldwide. By 1907, output would more than double.

1919 At the age of 75, and with his food factory one of the largest in America, Henry J. Heinz dies of pneumonia. He is succeeded by his son, Howard.

1925 The company went from strength to strength under the control of Howard. Branches began to open all over the world, including a large purpose-built factory in Harlesden, England, which would go on to survive two bombing attacks during the war.

1948 With the war ended, Heinz begins to produce Tomato Ketchup at a former munitions factory in the north-east English town of Standish.

1957 Heinz celebrate the year 1957 in style. With the '57 Varieties' tag to the fore, Heinz plastered the press with adverts for their products, even beginning a TV campaign on New Year's Day.

1972 The company passes the billion dollar sales mark.

1987 Heinz launch the plastic bottle with flip-top cap, an innovation that will enable their customers to get to their beloved ketchup quicker with one big squeeze!

2003 Heinz launch the Top Down bottle for instant application without any mess around the lid.

2006 Heinz Tomato Ketchup is 130 years old! Heinz launch the 'Have Your Say' promotion, inviting customers to create witty and creative labels for bottles of ketchup, eight of which, such as 'TAKE ME TO YOUR BURGER', made it into print, onto labels and onto retail shelves.

ACKNOWLEDGEMENTS

Firstly to Lynda, my wife, who has patiently shopped, written, washed up, cooked and re-cooked all these dishes with me, adding her special touch to make each recipe complete. A huge thanks to Paul Harvey at Heinz who encouraged me and gave me the privileged opportunity to write this book. Thank you to Andy Jones, a great chum and an excellent chef who has helped solve all sorts of technical foodie issues. And now thank you to my beloved labrador, Tiffy, who has stood by me for hours on end waiting for titbits to fall from my pans and to all those most precious friends and family who have served on my Heinz Tomato Ketchup tasting panels over many lunches and dinners.

Finally, to the help and encouragement from our publishers at Absolute Press, always there, always ready to guide and advise: thank you Jon, Meg and especially Matt, whose design and care has created such a fantastic book.

All food photography © Peter Cassidy.

Images on pages 30–31, 34, 36, 42, 43, 47 supplied by The History of Advertising Trust from the Heinz collection held at HAT.

Images on page 75: photography by Kevin Summers.

All other images courtesy of Heinz.

HERE'S TO ANOTHER

40...
50...
100...

GREAT KETCHUP EXPERIENCES